The Snake Olympics

Written by Mary-Anne Creasy

Illustrated by Alex Stitt

Flying Start
to Literacy®

Contents

Chapter 1: On your marks!

It was time for the Snake Olympics.
There were many events.

There would be an event to see which
snake could hide the best, and an event
to see which snake had the longest fangs.

And there would even be an event
to find the smartest hunter.

All the snakes were very excited
as they waited for
the Snake Olympics to begin.

They all wanted to win
the Snake Olympics.

The first event was to see which snake
was the best at hiding.

"Snakes, are you ready?" said the first
judge.   "The event is about to begin."

"I always win this," said the green tree snake as he slipped away to hide.

"They'll never find me,"
said the python as he slithered away.

One,
two,
three,
four,
five...

ZIP!
ZIP!
ZIP!

Chapter 2:
The best at hiding

The first judge climbed the tree.

"I can see you," he yelled,
as he nearly stepped on
the green tree snake.

"And I can see you too!" said the
second judge to the python curled
around the branch.

The second judge saw something wriggling in the leaves. It looked like a worm.

"What's that?" he said.

But when he went to have
a closer look, the death adder sprang
out from where it had been hiding.

"It's not a worm," said the first judge.
"It's the death adder."

"The death adder is the best
at hiding," said the judges.

11

Chapter 3:
The longest fangs

The next event was to see which snake had the longest fangs.

All the snakes smiled.

"Look at my fangs," said the puff adder, as he smiled his biggest smile.

"Those fangs are very big indeed," said the second judge nervously.

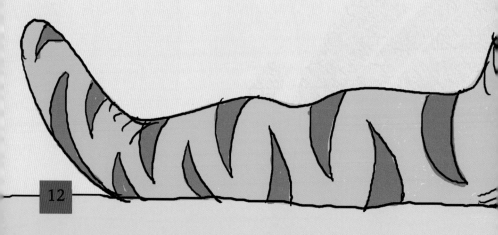

"I can beat him,"
said the gaboon viper.

She smiled at the judges and
showed her huge, long fangs.

The judges did not smile back.

"Look at those fangs!" they said.
"The gaboon viper wins the medal
for the longest fangs."

And they hurried off.

Chapter 4:
The smartest hunter

The next event was to find the smartest hunter.

"Each snake will try to catch a toy mouse," said the first judge. "The winner will be the snake who catches it in the smartest way."

"I'll win this one," said the python. The python slithered into the water and waited, with just his head showing.

The judge put the toy mouse on the ground and let it go. SPLASH!
The python sprang out of the water and grabbed the toy mouse as it sped past.

"Now it's my turn," said the puff adder.

The judge let the toy mouse go and it zoomed off.

The puff adder struck with amazing speed.

"Got you!" said the puff adder as
he grabbed the mouse.

"That was very, very fast,"
said the judges.

The next snake in the event was
the rattlesnake. He was blindfolded.

"You won't catch anything that way,"
sneered the python.

"Watch me," said the rattlesnake, and he
stayed very still as he waited for the mo

The mouse sped towards the rattlesnake.

The rattlesnake suddenly grabbed
the mouse in his mouth.

"The rattlesnake wins," said the judges.
"He's the smartest hunter."

Chapter 5:
Run for your life!

"Now I'll show you how fast
I am without my blindfold,"
said the rattlesnake.

But the judges didn't wait to find out!

A note from the author

When I started researching snakes, I thought they were all pretty much the same. But I discovered they are amazing animals, and most of them have something special about them. Just as I had decided that one snake had the longest fangs, a bit more research uncovered more information that revealed the gaboon viper has the longest fangs. It was almost like a competition in my research, which changed as more facts were uncovered. So I thought maybe the book itself could be a competition between the snakes: The Snake Olympics.